To I⋯

With love always

from

Granny & Grandad

xx

MINI CLASSICS

A CHILD'S GARDEN OF VERSES

A Parragon Book

Published by
Parragon Books,
Unit 13-17, Avonbridge Trading Estate,
Atlantic Road, Avonmouth, Bristol BS11 9QD.

Produced by
The Templar Company plc,
Pippbrook Mill, London Road, Dorking, Surrey RH4 1JE.

Copyright © 1994 Parragon Book Service Limited

Designed by Mark Kingsley-Monks

Printed and bound in Great Britain

ISBN 1-85813-645-8

A SELECTION FROM

A CHILD'S GARDEN OF VERSES

BY ROBERT LOUIS STEVENSON
ILLUSTRATED BY LESLEY SMITH

∥ •PARRAGON• ∥

TO ALISON CUNNINGHAM
FROM HER BOY

For the long nights you lay awake
And watched for my unworthy sake:
For your most comfortable hand
That led me through the uneven land:
For all the story-books you read:
For all the pains you comforted:
For all you pitied, all you bore,
In sad and happy days of yore:

—My second Mother, my first Wife,
The angel of my infant life—
From the sick child, now well and old,
Take, nurse, the little book you hold!

And grant it, Heaven that all who read
May find as dear a nurse at need,
And every child who lists my rhyme,
In the bright, fireside, nursery clime,
May hear it in as kind a voice
As made my childish days rejoice!

AT THE SEA-SIDE

When I was down beside the sea
A wooden spade they gave to me
To dig the sandy shore.

My holes were empty like a cup.
In every hole the sea came up,
Till it could come no more.

THE SWING

How do you like to go up in a swing,
Up in the air so blue?
Oh, I do think it the pleasantest thing
Ever a child can do!

Up in the air and over the wall,
Till I can see so wide,
Rivers and trees and cattle and all
Over the countryside—

Till I look down on the garden green,
Down on the roof so brown—
Up in the air I go flying again,
Up in the air and down!

YOUNG NIGHT THOUGHT

All night long and every night,
When my mama puts out the light,
I see the people marching by,
As plain as day, before my eye.

Armies and emperors and kings,
All carrying different kinds of things,
And marching in so grand a way,
You never saw the like by day.

So fine a show was never seen
At the great circus on the green;
For every kind of beast and man
Is marching in that caravan.

At first they move a little slow,
But still the faster on they go,
And still beside them close I keep
Until we reach the town of Sleep.

THE COW

The friendly cow all red and white,
I love with all my heart:
She gives me cream with all her might,
To eat with apple-tart.

She wanders lowing here and there,
And yet she cannot stray,
All in the pleasant open air,
The pleasant light of day;

And blown by all the winds that pass
And wet with all the showers,
She walks among the meadow grass
And eats the meadow flowers.

LOOKING-GLASS RIVER

Smooth it slides; upon its travel,
Here a wimple, there a gleam—
    O the clean gravel!
    O the smooth stream!

Sailing blossoms, silver fishes,
Paven pools as clear as air—
    How a child wishes
    To live down there!

We can see our coloured faces
Floating on the shaken pool
    Down in cool places,
    Dim and very cool;

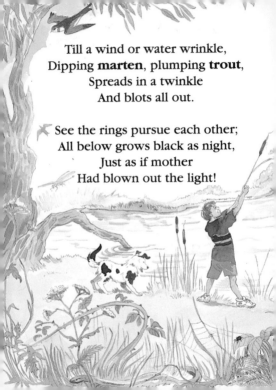

Till a wind or water wrinkle,
Dipping **marten**, plumping **trout**,
Spreads in a twinkle
And blots all out.

See the rings pursue each other;
All below grows black as night,
Just as if mother
Had blown out the light!

Patience, children, just a minute—
See the spreading circles die;
The stream and all in it
Will clear by-and-by.

PIRATE STORY

Three of us afloat
in the meadow by the swing,
Three of us aboard
in the basket on the lea.
Winds are in the air,
they are blowing in the spring,
And waves are on the meadow
like the waves there are at sea.

Where shall we adventure,
to-day that we're afloat,
Wary of the weather
and steering by a star?
Shall it be to Africa,
a-steering of the boat,
To Providence, or Babylon,
or off to Malabar?

Hi! but here's a squadron
a-rowing on the sea—
Cattle on the meadow
a-charging with a roar!
Quick, and we'll escape them,
they're as mad as they can be,
The wicket is the harbour
and the garden is the shore.

FOREIGN LANDS

Up into the cherry tree
Who should climb but little me?
I held the trunk with both my hands
And looked abroad on foreign lands.

I saw the next door garden lie,
Adorned with flowers, before my eye,
And many pleasant places more
That I have never seen before.

I saw the dimpling river pass
And be the sky's blue looking-glass;
The dusty roads go up and down
With people tramping into town.

If I could find a higher tree
Farther and farther I should see,
To where the grown-up river slips
Into the sea among the ships,

To where the roads on either hand
Lead onward into fairy land,
Where all the children dine at five,
And all the playthings come alive.

THE LAND OF NOD

From breakfast on through all the day
At home among my friends I stay,
But every night I go abroad
Afar into the land of Nod.

All by myself I have to go,
With none to tell me what to do—
All alone beside the streams
And up the mountain-sides of dreams.

The strangest things are there for me,
Both things to eat and things to see,
And many frightening sights abroad
Till morning in the land of Nod.

Try as I like to find the way,
I never can get back by day,
Nor can remember plain and clear
The curious music that I hear.

WINDY NIGHTS

Whenever the moon and stars are set,
Whenever the wind is high,
All night long in the dark and wet,
A man goes riding by.
Late in the night when the fires are out,
Why does he gallop and gallop about?

Whenever the trees are crying aloud,
And ships are tossed at sea,
By, on the highway, low and loud,
By at the gallop goes he.
By at the gallop he goes, and then
By he comes back at the gallop again.

MY SHADOW

I have a little shadow
that goes in and out with me,
And what can be the use of him
is more than I can see.
He is very, very like me
from the heels up to the head;
And I see him jump before me,
when I jump into my bed.

The funniest thing about him
is the way he likes to grow—
Not at all like proper children,
which is always very slow;
For he sometimes shoots up taller
like an india-rubber ball,
And he sometimes gets so little
that there's none of him at all.

He hasn't got a notion of
how children ought to play,
And can only make a fool of me
in every sort of way.
He stays so close beside me,
he's a coward you can see;
I'd think shame to stick to nursie
as that shadow sticks to me!

One morning, very early,
before the sun was up,
I rose and found the shining dew
on every buttercup;
But my lazy little shadow,
like an arrant sleepy-head,
Had stayed at home behind me
and was fast asleep in bed.

THE LAND OF COUNTERPANE

When I was sick and lay a-bed,
I had two pillows at my head,
And all my toys beside me lay
To keep me happy all the day.

And sometimes for an hour or so
I watched my leaden soldiers go,
With different uniforms and drills,
Among the bed-clothes, through the hills;

And sometimes sent my ships in fleets
All up and down among the sheets;
Or brought my trees and houses out,
And planted cities all about.

I was the giant great and still
That sits upon the pillow-hill,
And sees before him, dale and plain,
The pleasant land of counterpane.

The Wind

I saw you toss the kites on high
And blow the birds about the sky;
And all around I heard you pass,
Like ladies' skirts across the grass—
O wind, a-blowing all day long,
O wind, that sings so loud a song!

I saw the different things you did,
But always you yourself you hid.
I felt you push, I heard you call,
I could not see yourself at all—
O wind, a-blowing all day long,
O wind, that sings so loud a song!

O you that are so strong and cold,
O blower, are you young or old?
Are you a beast of field and tree,
Or just a stronger child than me?
O wind, a-blowing all day long,
O wind, that sings so loud a song!

FROM A RAILWAY CARRIAGE

Faster than fairies,
faster than witches,
Bridges and houses,
hedges and ditches;
And charging along
like troops in a battle,
All through the meadows
the horses and cattle:

All of the sights
of the hill and the plain
Fly as thick
as driving rain;
And ever again,
in the wink of an eye,
Painted stations
whistle by.

Here is a child
who clambers and scrambles,
All by himself
and gathering brambles;
Here is a tramp
who stands and gazes;
And there is the green
for stringing the daisies!
Here is a cart
run away in the road
Lumping along
with man and load;
And here is a mill
and there is a river:
Each a glimpse
and gone for ever!

A GOOD PLAY

We built a ship upon the stairs
All made of the back-bedroom chairs,
And filled it full of sofa pillows
To go a-sailing on the billows.

We took a saw and several nails,
And water in the nursery pails;
And Tom said, "Let us also take
An apple and a slice of cake;"—
Which was enough for Tom and me
To go a-sailing on, till tea.

We sailed along for days and days,
And had the very best of plays;
But Tom fell out and hurt his knee,
So there was no one left but me.

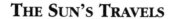

THE SUN'S TRAVELS

The sun is not a-bed, when I
At night upon my pillow lie;
Still around the earth his way he takes,
And morning after morning makes.

While here at home, in shining day,
We round the sunny garden play,
Each little Indian sleepy-head
Is being kissed and put to bed.

And when at eve I rise from tea,
Day dawns beyond the Atlantic Sea;
And all the children in the West
Are getting up and being dressed.

THE GARDENER

The gardener does not love to talk,
He makes me keep the gravel walk;
And when he puts his tools away,
He locks the door and takes the key.

Away behind the currant row
Where no one else but cook may go,
Far in the plots, I see him dig,
Old and serious, brown and big.

He digs the flowers, green, red, and blue,
Nor wishes to be spoken to.
He digs the flowers and cuts the hay,
And never seems to want to play.

Silly gardener! summer goes,
And winter comes with pinching toes,
When in the garden bare and brown
You must lay your barrow down.

Well now, and while the summer stays,
To profit by these garden days,
O how much wiser you would be
To play at Indian wars with me!

WHERE GO THE BOATS?

Dark brown is the river,
Golden is the sand.
It flows along for ever,
With trees on either hand.

Green leaves a-floating,
Castle of the foam,
Boats of mine a-boating—
Where will all come home?

On goes the river
And out past the mill,
Away down the valley,
Away down the hill.

Away down the river,
A hundred miles or more,
Other little children
Shall bring my boats ashore.

THE LAND OF STORY-BOOKS

At evening when the lamp is lit,
Around the fire my parents sit;
They sit at home and talk and sing,
And do not play at anything.

Now, with my little gun, I crawl
All in the dark along the wall,
And follow round the forest track
Away behind the sofa back.

There, in the night, where none can spy,
All in my hunter's camp I lie,
And play at books that I have read
Till it is time to go to bed.

These are the hills, these are the woods,
These are my starry solitudes;
And there the river by whose brink
The roaring lions come to drink.

I see the others far away
As if in firelit camp they lay,
And I, like to an Indian scout,
Around their party prowled about.

So, when my nurse comes in for me,
Home I return across the sea,
And go to bed with backward looks
At my dear land of Story-books.

AUTUMN FIRES

In the other gardens
And all up the vale,
From the autumn bonfires
See the smoke trail!

Pleasant summer over
And all the summer flowers,
The red fire blazes,
The grey smoke towers.

Sing a song of seasons!
Something bright in all!
Flowers in the summer,
Fires in the fall!

51

WINTER TIME

Late lies the wintry sun a-bed,
A frosty, fiery sleepy-head;
Blinks but an hour or two; and then,
A blood-red orange, sets again.

Before the stars have left the skies,
At morning in the dark I rise;
And shivering in my nakedness,
By the cold candle, bathe and dress.

Close by the jolly fire I sit
To warm my frozen bones a bit;
Or with a reindeer-sled, explore
The colder countries round the door.

When to go out, my nurse doth wrap
Me in my comforter and cap;
The cold wind burns my face, and blows
Its frosty pepper up my nose.

Black are my steps on silver sod;
Thick blows my frosty breath abroad;
And tree and house, and hill and lake,
Are frosted like a wedding-cake.

PICTURE-BOOKS IN WINTER

Summer fading, winter comes—
Frosty mornings, tingling thumbs,
Window robins, winter rooks,
And the picture story-books.

Water now is turned to stone
Nurse and I can walk upon;
Still we find the flowing brooks
In the picture story-books.

All the pretty things put by,
Wait upon the children's eye,
Sheep and shepherds, trees and crooks,
In the picture story-books.

We may see how all things are
Seas and cities, near and far,
And the flying fairies' looks,
In the picture story-books.

How am I to sing your praise,
Happy chimney-corner days,
Sitting safe in nursery nooks,
Reading picture story-books?

BLOCK CITY

What are you able
to build with your blocks?
Castles and palaces,
temples and docks.
Rain may keep raining,
and others go roam,
But I can be happy
and building at home.

Let the sofa be mountains,
the carpet be sea,
There I'll establish
a city for me:

A kirk and a mill
and a palace beside,
And a harbour as well
where my vessels may ride.

Great is the palace
with pillar and wall,
A sort of a tower
on the top of it all,
And steps coming down
in an orderly way
to where my toy vessels
lie safe in the bay.

This one is sailing
and that one is moored:
Hark to the song
of the sailors on board!
And see on the steps
of my palace, the kings
Coming and going
with presents and things!

Now I have done with it,
down let it go!
All in a moment
the town is laid low.
Block upon block
lying scattered and free,
What is there left
of my town by the sea?

Yet as I saw it,
I see it again,
The kirk and the palace,
the ships and the men,
And as long as I live
and where'er I may be,
I'll always remember
my town by the sea.

TRAVEL

I should like to rise and go
Where the golden apples grow:—
Where below another sky
Parrot islands anchored lie,
And, watched by cockatoos and goats,
Lonely Crusoes building boats;—
Where in sunshine reaching out
Eastern cities, miles about,
Are with mosque and minaret
Among sandy gardens set,
And the rich goods from near and far
Hang for sale in the bazaar;—

Where the Great Wall round China goes,
And on one side the desert blows,
And with bell and voice and drum,
Cities on the other hum;—
Where are forests, hot as fire,

Wide as England, tall as a spire,
Full of apes and cocoa-nuts
And the negro hunters' huts;—
Where the knotty crocodile
Lies and blinks in the Nile,
And the red flamingo flies
Hunting fish before his eyes;—

Where in jungles, near and far,
Man-devouring tigers are,
Lying close and giving ear
Lest the hunt be drawing near,
Or a comer-by be seen
Swinging in a palanquin;—
Where among the desert sands
Some deserted city stands,
All its children, sweep and prince,
Grow to manhood ages since,
Not a foot in street or house,

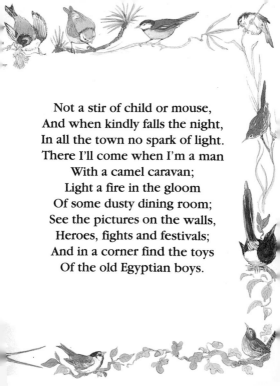

Not a stir of child or mouse,
And when kindly falls the night,
In all the town no spark of light.
There I'll come when I'm a man
With a camel caravan;
Light a fire in the gloom
Of some dusty dining room;
See the pictures on the walls,
Heroes, fights and festivals;
And in a corner find the toys
Of the old Egyptian boys.

NORTH-WEST PASSAGE
1. GOOD NIGHT

When the bright lamp is carried in,
The sunless hours again begin;
O'er all without, in field and lane,
The haunted night returns again.

Now we behold the embers flee
About the firelit hearth; and see
Our faces painted as we pass,
Like pictures, on the window-glass.

Must we to bed indeed? Well then,
   Let us arise and go like men,
And face with an undaunted tread
The long black passage up to bed.

Farewell, O brother, sister, sire!
O pleasant party round the fire!
The songs you sing, the tales you tell,
   Till far tomorrow, fare ye well!

MY SHIP AND I

O it's I that am the captain
of a tidy little ship,
Of a ship that goes a-sailing
on the pond;
And my ship it keeps a-turning
all around and all about;
But when I'm a little older,
I shall find the secret out
How to send my vessel
sailing on beyond.

73

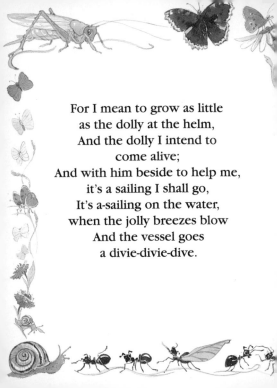

For I mean to grow as little
as the dolly at the helm,
And the dolly I intend to
come alive;
And with him beside to help me,
it's a sailing I shall go,
It's a-sailing on the water,
when the jolly breezes blow
And the vessel goes
a divie-divie-dive.

O it's then you'll see me sailing
through the rushes and the reeds,
And you'll hear the water
singing at the prow;
For beside the dolly sailor,
I'm to voyage and explore,
To land upon the island
where no dolly was before,
And to fire the penny cannon
in the bow.

MY KINGDOM

Down by a shining water well
I found a very little dell,
No higher than my head.
The heather and the gorse about
In summer bloom were coming out,
Some yellow and some red.

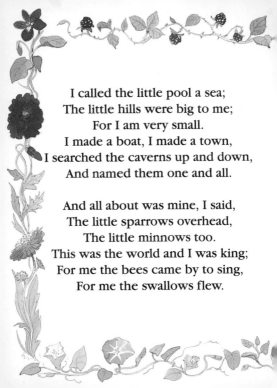

I called the little pool a sea;
The little hills were big to me;
For I am very small.
I made a boat, I made a town,
I searched the caverns up and down,
And named them one and all.

And all about was mine, I said,
The little sparrows overhead,
The little minnows too.
This was the world and I was king;
For me the bees came by to sing,
For me the swallows flew.

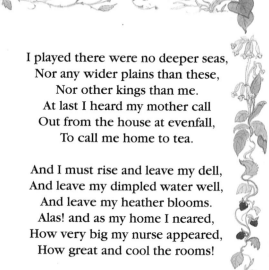

I played there were no deeper seas,
Nor any wider plains than these,
Nor other kings than me.
At last I heard my mother call
Out from the house at evenfall,
To call me home to tea.

And I must rise and leave my dell,
And leave my dimpled water well,
And leave my heather blooms.
Alas! and as my home I neared,
How very big my nurse appeared,
How great and cool the rooms!

THE MOON

The moon has a face
like the clock in the hall;
She shines on thieves
on the garden wall,
On streets and fields
and harbour quays,
And birdies asleep
in the forks of the trees.

The squalling cat
and the squeaking mouse,
The howling dog
by the door of the house,
The bat that lies
in bed at noon,
All love to be out
by the light of the moon.

But of all the things
that belong to the day
Cuddle to sleep
to be out of her way;
And flowers and children
close their eyes
Till up in the morning
the sun shall arise.

THE FLOWERS

All the names I know from nurse:
Gardener's garters, Shepherd's purse,
Bachelor's buttons, Lady's smock,
And the Lady Hollyhock.

Fairy places, fairy things,
Fairy woods where the wild bee wings,
Tiny trees for tiny dames—
These must all be fairy names!

Tiny woods below whose boughs
Shady fairies weave a house;
Tiny tree-tops, rose or thyme,
Where the braver fairies climb!

Fair are grown-up people's trees,
But the fairest woods are these;
Where if I were not so tall,
I should live for good and all.

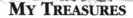

MY TREASURES

These nuts, that I keep
in the back of the nest
Where all my lead soldiers
are lying at rest,
Were gathered in autumn
by nursie and me
In a wood with a well
by the side of the sea.

This whistle we made
(and how clearly it sounds!)
By the side of a field
at the end of the grounds.
Of a branch of a plane,
with a knife of my own,
It was nursie who made it,
and nursie alone!

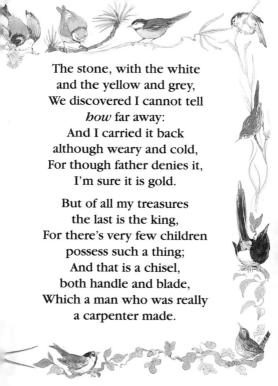

The stone, with the white
and the yellow and grey,
We discovered I cannot tell
how far away:
And I carried it back
although weary and cold,
For though father denies it,
I'm sure it is gold.

But of all my treasures
the last is the king,
For there's very few children
possess such a thing;
And that is a chisel,
both handle and blade,
Which a man who was really
a carpenter made.

ESCAPE AT BEDTIME

The lights from the parlour
and kitchen shone out
Through the blinds and
the windows and bars;
And high overhead
and all moving about,
There were thousands of
millions of stars.
There ne'er were such thousands
of leaves on a tree,
Nor of people in church or the Park,
As the crowds of the stars
that looked down upon me,
And that glittered
and winked in the dark.

The Dog, and the Plough,
and the Hunter, and all,
And the star of the sailor, and Mars,
These shone in the sky,
and the pail by the wall
Would be half full of water and stars.
They saw me at last,
and they chased me with cries,
And they soon had me packed into bed;
But the glory kept shining
and bright in my eyes,
And the stars going round in my head.

TO ANY READER

As from the house your mother sees
You playing round the garden trees,
So you may see, if you will look
Through the windows of this book
Another child, far, far away,
And in another garden, play.
But do not think you can at all,
By knocking on the window, call

That child to hear you. He intent
Is all on his play-business bent.
He does not hear; he will not look,
Nor yet be lured out of this book.
For, long ago, the truth to say,
He has grown up and gone away,
And it is but a child of air
That lingers in the garden there.

ROBERT LOUIS STEVENSON

Robert Louis Stevenson was born on
November 13th, 1850 in Edinburgh, Scotland
and is one of the 19th century's best-loved
storytellers. *Treasure Island* was written for his
12 year old stepson, Samuel, and was followed
by adventures such as *Kidnapped* and
The Strange Case of Dr Jekyll and Mr Hide.
A Child's Garden of Verses was written
over the period 1884–86 from his sickbed; the
writer was dogged by ill-health for much of his
life. Offering a glimpse of childhood memories,
these delightful poems capture the hearts of
each new generation as it enjoys afresh the
child's innocent delight in simple pleasures and
discoveries. Robert Louis Stevenson died in 1894
and was buried under his own epitaph:
"Here he lies where he long'd to be;
Home is the sailor, home from the sea,
And the hunter home from the hill."